EYES IN THE WOOD:

OCCASIONAL PROSE

Eleanor Rees is the author of *Portents and Portals: New & Selected Poems* (Guillemot, 2024), and five collections of poetry including *Andraste's Hair*, shortlisted for the Forward Prize for Best First Collection. Eleanor is the recipient of an Eric Gregory Award, Northern Writers' Award and her poems have been translated into Lithuanian, Slovak, French, German, Romanian and Spanish (Versopolis, 2016, 2019, 2024). She is a senior lecturer in creative writing at Liverpool Hope University and lives on the Wirral peninsula, UK.

Also by Eleanor Rees

CONTENTS

ISBN: 978-1-917617-28-4

Cover designed by Aaron Kent

Edited by Alice Brooker

Typeset by Aaron Kent

Broken Sleep Books Ltd
PO BOX 102
Llandysul
SA44 9BG

Eyes in the Wood

Eleanor Rees

Broken Sleep Books

INTRODUCTION

THIS collection draws together prose writings about poetry written between 2014 and 2025. The writings here are responses to specific publishing contexts such as a preface, blog or online article. The occasional quality of these prose writings offers an engagement with contemporary posthuman and new-materialist philosophy through the practice of a contemporary poet in the edgelands and peripheries of England, Wales and Europe.

The intention here is to preserve these transient articulations of the ideas informing my poetics and offer a broader intellectual contribution to contemporary thought. I include two lyric essays to this end.

My writings in poetry and prose can be understood as encounters with poiesis, a response to the generative, lively potential of the world and a valuation of life in times of crisis.

EYES IN THE WOOD :
HOW TO KNOW A WORLD WHICH IS
ALWAYS LOOKING BACK?

ON the banks of the River Mersey at Cressington Park esplanade, low tide, sandbanks rising, crows peck along the waterline. I look across to Eastham Ferry on the edge of the Wirral Peninsula, to green woods and a white building, once a hotel, cwtched into the dark trees. The view beyond leans into the Clywdian hills where a brightness frames the distance. Grey clouds balance along the ridge like a scale, hold equilibrium as the river flows towards and in; the sea to the west loosening its grip and the towers of Stanlow oil refinery dragging waves to the east. A hammer taps this shore; a man behind a garden wall, behind me, trims the already-neatened hedge.

I have come here to look back at the old white hotel and meet its gaze. I can see the frontage from every walk I take on this side of the river. I have come here to think about knowing, to write in my recycled notebooks in blue scrawling ink, whatever happens in the act of looking back. I can only do this when I am on the edge of my city, Liverpool. I will tie all the strands together later, on a computer, finding meaning in my improvisations and in that binding action, question and learn. I am trying to describe how I think as a poet and writer; how the knowledge gleaned within being becomes a poem; how a non-linear conception of time and space is not a representation, a false imagining but an engagement with the entanglement of the world. Starting from an ontology which isn't linear or neat requires an atunement to how meanings shift, change and transform within subjectivity and how being presents these to the mind as meaningful: steppingstones within the peat. Poetic thought in practice is an act of stepping sideways, or leaping over decaying branches, or digging through the ground. I have to go around, over and through, down into as I am always within the thought. I can't just count the leaves on the tree or cut it up into tiny pieces whilst feeling powerful about its subservience to my mind and method: O how sharp is my axe. Hubris will lead to false knowledge, parts not systems, dominance understood as truth rather than the defensive act it is. Truth isn't dominant, it is wide-open and more-than-human.

*

To write about looking back I will write about my ancestors. One of my earliest memories, or a memory I've come to name as such, is seeing the 'eyes in the wood', the wood-panelled walls of a Victorian vicarage on the edge of a small post-industrial town in Lancashire. My grandfather was an Anglo-Catholic, Anglo Welsh vicar from a family of four generations of clergy, beginning in South Wales on the Gower Peninsula in the 1840s. I can now see again the exterior in my mind's eye, though my memory is of how the dark wooden interior looked back towards a toddler running from study, to living room, to kitchen in a loop. Each room had connecting doors which enabled this flow. My grandfather peeled an apple in one corkscrew move: no breaks. I have always understood objects as living phenomena, looking back into my gaze.

And raising my eyes again, I meet the white hotel, or the muddy grey, small, tamed presence encircled by trees to its back and the wash of silver to its front. In the Rees family archive of 19th century letters, lectures, drawings and scrapbook is a letter written by Rev. William Davidson Wood-Rees, my great, great grandfather to his mother on the occasion of his honeymoon. I read it in May 2020, and now it is two years later, and only now do I feel I can speak with his thoughts. They have settled in me, fleshed out in images. I intended to quote his words here in this essay, to amplify his words across time. But in practice, in the first draft of this text, I left silences, told myself I just didn't want to risk taking the letter out of the plastic folder in the storage box, risk dirtying its fragile surfaces. I let his voice sing only as placeholder hashtags in the gaps in the sentences and so, from memory, invoke what I have read to reanimate his words in mine.

Do I have my ancestor's permission to quote his words from an intimate letter written to his mother kept quiet in a box for two hundred years, reanimated only by his descendant's eyes, perhaps once a generation? How would I feel if in two hundred years' time my private letters were quoted in public? On reflection, I'd hate it. I felt this recognition as a force, the boundary between private and public, ink and speech, a form. I will not steal Wood-Rees' words, cajole them into my own meanings, but animate them through my body, transform them through my own speech.

*

Wood-Rees is standing on the water's edge, looking back towards me. It is 1879 and he has travelled on the steamer from Liverpool

Pierhead landing stage to the pleasure gardens downriver as part of his honeymoon, walking now with his love in the green woods. He sees the training ships in the Mersey and almost sees me looking back at him across the moon-drawn river. Wood-Rees writes about his trip to Eastham Ferry pleasure gardens in his letter to his mother that I read one warm May Day in 2020, unable to go outside due to Covid lockdown. Wood-Rees speaks to me through my astonishment that he also walked the roads I know and write, also crossed the river I've always crossed; that traces of me were here before I came to be; that my memories linger and shiver now, carried in his body, also finding their way into his own life, drawing together here in my gaze at the edge of the river towards Eastham Ferry and the blur of the white hotel.

I have not visited Eastham Ferry, only looked back at it, since I was a child when dad took myself, my sister and two friends to walk in the woods on a rainy autumnal half-term; four girls in bright 80s macs, and we found the bear pit in the disused pleasure gardens, surrounded by a muddy path and the remains of a trail, and climbed down and in; and I looked up in the body of a bear and was caught, and breathless and full of rage for his suffering, for the bear was lonely and old, and crying, as bears do, deep inside his fur and his bellows, a silent roar; and children roam around his ghost; I felt his sorrow deep like a pit without an end, a pit I was trapped in; sandstone black mossy walls; how his body had become a possession, an ownership of teeth, a white of the eye and transportations in crates, small boxes, and meat for his food uncaught or trapped but thrown and rotten; and Wood-Rees walks past in love on May Day full of the rush of spring air and the chime of the bells and I am no longer a bear, or a ghost, or my ancestor walking, or my dad also sorrowful that day I think, or even standing on the far side of the river but returning to the esplanade, the agony of the bear's enclosure in my eyes' wet, a fierce impulse to set him loose, to let him rip up my arm, to find a log to create an escape, to let the bear free in the pleasure gardens to hide and cower in the woods; as Wood-Rees mounts the tram to the ferry and does not see him, or my face looking back across the water as the wheels of the tram squeak into flow and he moves on.

The bear runs wild into the woodland, unseen also, turning his wet eyes back to see no-one see, or look, or watch his body – no human, not his fur-bound shape – as he rushes to the mountains and is free.

Later, in a different wood, I see the bear for a moment on the edge of the trees, a furry, soft back slips into the bark and then becomes squirrel on the woodland floor at the base of the tree, hazelnut in paw, teeth working tightly across the shell.

"You didn't need to leave me, you could stay. Let's speak a while in this green wood."

*

In imaginative thought, I can think within the entanglements of being. Imagination understood as a capacity to perceive the world in many dimensions, to shift beyond a static first-person point of view but move between, across, within and through space and time. The first-person view can move within the terrain finding alternative forms of relation afforded by the special limits of visionary thought. Rather than conceiving of this experience as fantastical or false, this form of perception is truthful; reason and imagination are entangled as a way of knowing as reason is a response to consequences apprehended in the mind's eye. To know a world which is always looking back is to dispense with the modern separation of reason and imagination and then actively embrace both in pursuit of knowledge in motion.

Anthropologist, Tim Ingold, in his essay 'Dreaming of Dragons' repairs the separation between imagination and reason, necessary as 'cutting imagination adrift from its earthly moorings and leaving it to float like a mirage above the road we tread in our material life' has had 'fateful consequences' for 'human life and habitation'. (Ingold: 2021, p 62) The modern 'self-evident' divide between reason and imagination leads to questions about how to reconcile the two. Yet in asking these questions Ingold argues, we 'forget, how hard it is, in our experience, to split the reality of our life in the world, and the world in which we live, from the mediative currents of our imagination.' (p.62). Ingold writes from an ontological understanding which does not separate reason and imagination and he describes examples from across cultures, drawing on Medieval English monastic life and the indigenous ontology of the Canadian Ojibwa people. Both medieval dragons and the thunderbird of the Ojibwa are understood to be real, as their existence has an agency, an impact on the humans who sees them and know them, and it is this interaction and communion with the imagined which confers their ontological status as real creatures. The conjured presence is known in an imagined relation,

Listening and responding to thunder is a matter not of a translation but of empathy, of establishing a communion of feeling and affect or, in short of opening oneself up to the being of another. And it is above all in dreaming, where the boundaries that surround the self in waking life are dissolved, that this opening occurs. (p.67)

For dreaming of dragons or thunderbirds allows existence to be known fulsomely and richly, 'in this quest for knowledge through experience, the powerful more-that-human beings…are not analogical resources but vital interlocutors.' (p.67) A human person needs to listen to the world beyond themselves and allow life space to live, to have agency and power, beyond the boundaried and frozen conception of the humanist self; the world is known as part of the becoming of the subjectivity of the interlocutor. We are the

communion between world and self, subject and object, the inter-
stices.

*

I have come to the river again to ask the bear what he has to say.

"I am the rain, this light drizzle, now lifting across the still lake of
the river, tide-absent and dosing- flat", he says, "I became the fog",
he says, a bear bright eye shining through the cloud, and I look out
as the tier of mist rises from the water as the sun arrives, as a white
van turns the corner of the esplanade, and the cold evaporates into
birdsong. Towards me, though the hotel beyond is shaded by cloud,
the Clwydian hills rest lower today, melded into a ridge of cloud and
the bear walks along their ridge, flitting into sight and out.

Eastham Ferry landing stage, I read last night, was built to
receive tourists, Victorian day trippers arriving on the pleasure
steamer from the Pierhead (30-45 mins away) and the hotel held
balls and afternoon teas; and ships' captains slept there on the way
up the Manchester Ship Canal and on to Salford Quays. A circus
performed in the saw dust ring, visitors sitting on the grassy bank
watching tightrope walkers and dancing bears.

O my bear, forgive us.

He turns his head into the rain.

"Never," he says, "The pain was searing and your disrespect so
loud."

Wood-Rees today still walks along the trails admiring the musi-
cians and the statues. He is newly- married, about to travel to Barmby Moor, to live in that same village forever – though he is always
here, and, also there, buried under the wheatgrass along the road
from North Wood House, its stables, his collection of mammoth
teeth, his dark wood carvings.

In the scrapbook of writings by Wood-Rees, a newspaper article celebrates him at 80, describes his private museum which contains a prehistoric women's skull found in a local field. He is a believer in 'dreams, telepathic and inspired', lives surrounded by 'beautiful carvings' made from a linen press and a bedstead, a screen which now stands in my hall on which he displayed his finds. Wood-Rees is of 'Welsh ancestry' and remembers Carmarthenshire communal singing as a youth. In a published story for a newspaper, he writes about a parson who, exhausted from working in the slums, falls in love with a woman on a train only to lose her and then find her injured in a hospital. She recovers and they live happily ever after, working for the needs of the poor. Imagination pervades all aspects of his life as he gathers time around him and speaks across the divide with the dying and the dead.

As I look up, Wood-Rees looks back at the far shore where I stand notebook in hand, a smudge of large white villas with portico windows and four chimneys on the huge stacks which air the fires in the many rooms where women sit inside and watch the sun outside the window brightening – we can see the same sun, searching across the mud to show its details. He walks in the green wood; behind is the bear who weeps in restricted sorrow, feels scratched with adrenaline, and the need to fight tire his abused body. The bear winces. I want to hold him.

And Wood-Rees will travel home then on the tram to see the May Day Parade in Castle Street, central Liverpool, horses and carts hung with oranges, the scent so visceral and exact it travels across time in his phrasing as I read the letter and it stays with me across the years it has taken me to begin to write this essay.

But looking back towards his future as he parades through pleasure gardens, his new wife on an arm, his imagination ringing like mine does with music, words, and scent, he will go to visit his brother. I look downriver to where the ridge lengthens over Birkenhead and Camel Lairds shipyard facing the still waters without a ship to launch. In the trees is the green woods, behind Birkenhead Park, newly opened, is St Anselm's College, training school for the ministry and those without means to go to university. There his brother Glyn lies in a bed in a dormitory, poorly but recovering, waiting for an evening visit, as yet now undetermined and unknown, communicated in a telegram sent hours later to take Wood-Rees again across the river to visit him. As he sails on the ferry, Wood Rees looks back downstream from the open deck and to the esplanade where I stand, out-of-sight, turning my head back towards the morning and the gulls' cries.

*

How then does a subject know an object which is always looking back? I need to listen. This lessens my solidity to create inner space for the emergence of otherness within the spaces between aspects of my selves. The identified self, the social self must stand back, not appropriate or project, but shift into, to carry some traces forward, and yet leave some aspects of the self behind. This energetic shift is a real movement of matter happening in time and space. Some of the subject stays still, some of it moves, stretches, morphs but maintains its coherence; does not break but bends and curves. Within this monistic view of being, matter shifts into another state but also retains its present form. Empathy isn't a state of presence but is a momentary absence. Poetic thought is also an emptying out of the self to allow for other meanings to emerge.

How does this occur? Through movement, repetition, improvisation. My return to the same spot on the esplanade to write this lyric prose, to look to the same focus on the horizon to steady my gaze, to drink hot tea from a flask, to write on a white blank page in scrawling blue. To steady my mind in description, in the moment of choosing language which enacts for me the thought, brings association but also is chosen due to the sound, the rhythm of a sentence which rings out from an internal voice linking silently into my gut, a controlling of my breath as if I am about to sing, a letting go into the constraints of all my daily thoughts to find the language jangling along of its own accord; a voice emerging out of this state which is not driven by personal needs but is a softening, relaxing into and over the other anxieties of the daily self and invoking, through conjuring in the mind's vision, aspects of the self beyond the self. To think 'with' is to know the world as a looking back, as animate as 'I', and to connect with it requires an emptying of the humanistic self, into what is more-than-human.

Yet this emptying must be carefully navigated as it is not a dive down into negativity. Within my philosophic schema, there is no negativity as pure absence, only a lessening of intensity to allow for something to enter the space, for the outside to blow in. This is not a conflict between two states, positive and negative, but a relation more like the tide I see as I stand by the river, always powerful, sometimes high, sometimes low. Neither is a pejorative or an aspiration.

An ethical relation created across difference needs to retain a value for boundaries. Traipsing over other people's self-definition is a hierarchical response. No means no. Resistance requires form, shape, and structure. Resistance must be known to be firm. Yet there are many ways of knowing, and imaginative thought offers a form of perception which focuses on shape and spaces in context; situated but not static, rather than deductive abstractions built on logics of dissection or acquisitive transgressions. Imaginative thought is not an engagement with nothingness, but an engagement with pattern, texture, shape, and space. By thinking with these forms, power relationships become liminal for a moment; not a tussle but a hybridising, both sides lose, and both can gain. This happens within imagination, a virtual edgeland.

*

Looking back doesn't always offer the answers required for the present, if by looking back the narrative we see is linear and reductive. To know a subject which is always looking back, the concept of time needs to be reconceptualised and not understood as a linear formation or a narrative progression from simplicity to complexity. By rethinking time in relation to place and choosing to look over and across rather than backwards, origin myths are avoided, and humanness is understood in terms of continuous human capacities, both pre and post human, as potentialities which have always been present become visible again, once unacknowledged and now seen; heads were turned backwards, stretching necks to see into the mist. Time and space are in literal flux. When we look back, we also look forwards.

The Welsh culture which lived on in the Anglo-Catholicism of my grandfathers as a valuing of myth, poetry and the otherworld wasn't centred on the human or on ideas of progress. However, it also wasn't simply regressive. Wood-Rees preached within the Church of England, but some of his ideas and writings can be interpreted as traces of a Welsh rural culture and its alternative ways of knowing. In his sermon on marriage, reported in The Daily Chronicle, Wood- Rees's respect and desire to protect women's intellect can be understood as a critique of his perception of modern attitudes to marriage which 'in the materialistic age' led men to marry 'bodies, ignoring beauty of soul, mind and intellect'. I wonder if this could be thought a lingering cultural trace of the Medieval Welsh Hywel laws which offered more 'rights' to women relative to the times?

Historian John Davies writes, 'the (Hywel) law is among the most splendid creations of the customs of the Welsh.... it is folk law rather than state law and its emphasis was upon reconciliation between kinship groups rather than upon keeping order through punishment.' (p.86) Davies continues that it has been shown that, 'it contained elements of mercy, common sense and respect for women and children which would be lacking in the law of England until very recently.' (p.84) He also writes that, 'It is plausible that the meeting to consolidate the Law was... held at Whitland.' (p84) The town of Whitland is in Carmarthenshire just south of the village of Llanboidy where Wood-Rees's grandfather was born. David Rees moved to Carmarthen, a few miles from Whitland, to become a tallow chandler, raising Wood-Rees's father, Rev. George Edgar Rees in the town. Wood-Rees also spent time as a boy living in Carmarthenshire when his family moved back due to his father's ill health. Is it possible Wood-Rees grew up in a society which still contained traces of these laws which would differ from the attitudes to women found in England?

Wood-Rees's attitude to the human place in the cosmos also appears contemporary as he held on to another notion of time within the shadow of the teleology of the orthodox church. His sense of time and place were never colonised into humanism. In an article from The Daily Chronicle, possibly written in 1930s, about his private museum, Wood-Rees is understood as not interpreting archaeological finds as proof of human dominance over nature but as evidence for a sense of scale and avoidance of hubris, 'In comparison with the period of time bridged by the bones of the tiny Bronze Age woman, which he keeps carefully wrapped up in a small box, his own span of life has come to seem of small account'. The journalist is careful to present Wood- Rees as a modest man which is also my impression of his character as I imagine him as I read his scrapbooks, his lectures and letters.

*

When writing, I am not writing to convey meaning already known but using the practice of writing as a way of knowing. The connection between mind and body in this moment is found in the lyric tone of this prose; an emergence in the moment, working with the flow of language as it produces a sense of self. Yet this moment is not a dissolution, or a fall into negativity, for I am not writing with extremes, with poles pitted against each other, but following a monistic imagining of matter which I find myself in the middle of, navigating but not fully in control of what comes to be. I have not 'lost myself' as myself didn't exist as a solid presence prior to this moment but I am more fully myself here, able to loosen into a fluidity which can reach over and beyond the limits imposed by social norms. This inner freedom is light and energising, pulling my perceptions over into the flush of the water. But in this flow rational thought is not lost. The need to find words, to think with them and keep true to the impulse of the syntax means I am patterning myself into the language. I am noticing what is happening around me, drawing these observations into my rendering of the moment on the page. I am giving life space to become enworded.

To do this means I am not only present in my body, but I am also in conversation with my thinking self which maintains a distance and witnesses the world around this moment of composition. I am not immersed or lost as some might frame this moment. I am travelling in it, riding in it, not submitting to the strong desire to leave my body and fly into the water and become with it. The language is a harness which keeps hold of the form of a self as I travel outside and into the distance, across space and time and layers of myself. When I reach an image, the bear, my relative, I can choose to step into their porous skin or stand alongside them and engage with them from the outside. Entering their flesh and bone, means my body also shakes and shivers. I am crying as I write about the entrapment of the bear; I carry with me anxieties about the restrictions of selfhood our limited society places on us; how this frustrates and confuses yet this isn't my experience, I am projecting onto the bear. I am aware of the look in his eyes, his shabby fur. My knowledge of animal care from a life outside of academia, from a youth spent riding horses, tells me this animal is unwell. I want to heal this unreal animal.

The bear does not stand in for something else. The bear is not a representation, though part of my mind knows he could be read as this and plays to this audience. Yet in the imaginative moment of the meeting across the water in the bear pit all I can sense is the suffering and an overwhelming need to become that energy and bring it new energy; to readdress the imbalance with new fuel or new heat or with energy I've brought from the power of the river's flow to pour this into the form of the bear until it is wild again and fierce, able to escape these bounds made for it by those that seek to control our fire.

*

Today the wind is strong and blowing from the east. The high tide has risen and is now depleting itself, returning to the ocean in an enthusiastic rush, and looking up, I can see the whole of the hotel facing me directly today, no mist or cloud and only the outline of Wales on the horizon line, two humps of hills and a valley reeling away towards the winds.

The bear is in his pit and crying. Wood-Rees is preparing to leave for Yorkshire. He doesn't walk out in the green wood but packs his bags inland in lodgings on Edge Lane and waits to get the steam train north... but no – look – there static on the wave, a small rowing boat oaring its way, and in it Wood-Rees – his face turned to me and waving – it bobs on the centre of the river where the sandbanks are emerging and a crow flies over lifting me, yes, up and then down to see him again, just like the photo on the stairs of our house when I was small. I'd leap past his eyes' stare, there and also here – but there he is as bright as the slivery grey swish of the river – and in the boat in the stern sits the bear who raises his nose to the wind and the tide has risen again; around the green wood is an island and the bear lives on amongst the trees writing songs sung to the breeze. O we need to listen and look differently to what is also there, amongst the waves.

And Wood-Rees looks back at the bear and then turns his boat against the waves, oaring against the tide towards the island which has risen amongst the pools of the Wirral. And he climbs ashore, watches the ships sail, the trams rust and scrap, his wife rides the train to Barmby Moor with half of his heart; and a self he almost didn't see clambers down into the pit, sits amongst the stones, as the bear runs free in the wild wood and the ivy grows over the sandstone. Wood-Rees crouches, waiting for me to come to meet him eye-to-eye in the darkness as he prays and I look up, mouthing "sorry, forgive me" to the island where a council of bears meets under where the Triumphal Arch used to stand and the bears are asked to vote on our culpability. From the bench on the far shore, I watch their paws rising, "yes," they say "yes". So, on the island we remain, surrounded by the waves as the eyes of the bears look back and listen to our pleas.

On the eighth day, they say we can leave – that our penance is past, that I should never cross the river or come to this place again, I should carry the pain they felt in their paws and teeth, in their ragged coats and hurt will crush through us every time the tide rises and the air cools. Wood-Rees hails a tram, gets the train east with his new wife to Barmby Moor.

I step into the waves and walk, not looking back.

*

In my rented hallway, nailed for stability to the magnolia wallpaper, is a wooden screen I also inherited from my grandparents. The screen is carved with mythological figures. A man holds a baby with a lion's head, another two figures carry two decapitated heads, another has the head of a bird, legs like a man and wings. There are two lions with wings also. It is hard to know from where in the world these figures originate. The screen was carved by hand by Rev. Wood-Rees in Barmby Moor around the late 1800s, early 1900s. In a clipping from a newspaper article from The Daily Chronicle the journalist reports that Wood-Rees carved the screen to display his collection of archaeological finds from the Yorkshire fields around his village. My dad thinks Wood-Rees found the images in books. As Wood-Rees's descendant and also woodworker and maker, I think my dad may well be right. In the newspaper article, the journalist says Wood-Rees made the screen from an old linen chest and a bedstead. The screen has curved shelving at the front which would support this account. The work involved is considerable. Carving the screen must have taken days, weeks, months. An enquiry to the Principal Curator, St Fagans National Museum of History confirmed, 'There is a long tradition of wood carving in Wales, dating back to the medieval period and up to more recent times, seen on various objects such as furniture, lovespoons and Eisteddfod chairs.' (Williams). I see the screen as a Welsh object. It is Welsh Folk Art though made in Yorkshire.

I can see Wood-Rees leant over the screen in North Wood House, the vicarage at Barmby Moor, chiselling away on long winter afternoons. He is leaning into the wood; the chisel slicing into the linen chest to create shapes and forms otherworldly to my ancestor's eyes. Ingold writes that making is about communing with the material, seeing what can be found in the shape of the stone, not imposing a hylomorphic model on the material. (Ingold, p 210-212) Wood-Rees is, I think, protecting the ancient, valuing other ways of seeing and knowing in his communion with this wood. To carve is to work with, to come alongside the material and to find form inside it. Wood-Rees leans in more closely, energetically moving eye from image to wood to eye and hand and in this he is absorbed, the creatures on the screen becoming part of him in the motion as the edges between human, wood, and culture blur into the action. In his reverie, he knows the reality of these more-than-human creatures. They speak and walk and stare back into his eyes as he chisels them into the world. He is acting out his fascination with an ancient imaginary and in doing so becoming the past in the present. A different cultural way of knowing he intuits needs to be conserved and remembered, is in danger of erasure in his journey through British cultures, from Welsh to English, Swansea clerk to Yorkshire priest.

*

Knowledge is becoming, not representation. Knowledge is alive. To know the world, we must become another aspect of the world, experience being from the inside, in the spaces created through matter's continual emergence. Beginning with a horizontal ontology, a piece of wood laid out on a workbench, we become the wood through our close attention and our actions, not copying but responding to what is already there and here. The subject isn't separate from the wood to begin with but already entangled at a physical level, so the separation can be understood as a form of illusion. Yet the definitions made by life to matter are essential and inevitable. The subject exists in a form in relation to other shapes. Thinking physically in space and time is meaningful; thought is a lived experience. By noticing the shape, the pattern, the gesture, we replicate and enact, try out a different shape for a while to see how the world feels from a different perspective. I find this happens to me without my choosing, sometimes slipping into spaces which exist in the shadows of an old building, or in the tone of a conversation. This isn't empathy as such, imagining a coherent emotional state and echoing that, but something more abstract, a taking on of the skin of the world, becoming wood, becoming otherly creature, powerful and energetic. Shapeshifting is erotic and loving, a communion with the living world in which one form swells into another.

Shapeshifting is not appropriating a representation to claim it as one's own; it is not ownership, for this state of attention changes the subject, myself; and knowledge is not known as a result, taken, and consumed, but understood through acting out. This can only be done if boundaries are respected, shape is maintained, that which is being known holds its power and coherence. Subject and object must be in balance. Form does not dissolve, fragment, or die but is conserved as form from which to build other forms, linen-chest to mythical screen, movement of light to lyric poem.

The subject which is looking back is exalted by the gaze, not reduced, seen with as much clarity and care as can be brought by the looker, for the gaze arises from a mutable subject, not a fixed presence, an opening into the space to take on dimensions, ridges, dust and light and to allow those attributes to work through consciousness to make another pattern, a variation on the same; each a new iteration. By seeing difference, we also see similarity. To be asked to value sameness over difference, and difference over sameness is a false dichotomy. Theirs is an entanglement without binary relation and to know it is to acknowledge this monastic principle. To acknowledge is to accept and recognise, that as in carving or when writing a poem, making one change to the form alters the next move and the next. One action or choice is always many.

And to think beyond binaries within entanglement and paradox we need to use imagination, not understood as newness, but as visioning, poetic vision even, which is a thinking with and through all aspects of the question, its shape, form, sense and affects, associations, luxuriating and turning as in water, until the waves still or bob to shore; or a screen is carved with enthusiasm and love for alternative ways of knowing, such as a way of valuing one's fading heritage inside an identity which asks for some formations of yourself to be abandoned; or a view is observed and brought to life through the complex action of looking back.

'DUSK TOWN' AND 'CONGLETON TAPESTRY': WRITING WITH SMALL TOWNS

GROWING up in a post-industrial northern town in the 1980s and 1990s I can see the potential in post-industrial environments, not just the loss. When I was invited to give readings in two libraries in small towns in Cheshire I felt a fascination and pleasure at the work involved. Seeing the value where others might not is part of the challenge of local poetics. Here was an opportunity to stretch my interpretative skills. I was excited by the landscapes: disused factories, canals, boarded up houses; the remains of industry, yet immanent, like seed. Runcorn is a town which has always caught my attention from the train travelling south across the railway bridge. Runcorn functions in my imaginary map of home as the gateway town: the boundary crossing back over the grace of the Mersey and into the familiar. Congleton however was a place I had never visited. It is located to the south-west of the Cheshire Plain on the edge of the Pennines, near Stoke. I had to find it on the map.

I was to write as a local poet but as an outsider. The risks were high. The expectation was I would read each poem at an evening event in the libraries to promote the reading of poetry. I had originally been invited to read already published work so had increased the stakes by offering this project. The audience would be local library users, so most likely long-standing residents of these towns. In the few weeks I had to write the poems I had to make sure I caught the current mood of the place, its aspirations and problems and also get the facts right. Yet the poem needed to have integrity and be a piece of work comparable with my other published poetry. The poem needed to be creative and engaging yet sensitive to its context. My self-created 'local problem' was in need of a 'local solution'. The material forces at work here needed attention. I had to attune to the expectations of the librarians, potential audience and also the places themselves. The agency of the river, the houses, the local history I learnt as stories had to come alive in me, inside my imagination. To invoke this occurrence I apply self-generated pressure. Research is crucial; yet not just reading about the place but experiential, visiting, looking, walking, building to a critical mass of stimuli. My energy levels have to rise until I am carrying almost too much information. I become overwhelmed with competing needs and from this pressure to create space for the excess of feeling, the affect of the environment and the relationships, I will begin to visualise other versions of places. The poem will begin to emerge.

In Runcorn at Halton Lea Library I attended a reminiscence afternoon with local older people in the refurbished library in the 1970s shopping centre. I was shown slides of important moments in Runcorn's past: the building of the bridge, the transporter taking cars across the river, barge people working on the Brindley and Manchester Ship Canal. I was able to talk with the group about their memories and glean, by making extensive notes and analysing them later, what was important to the community. I looked for similarities, repeated phrases and terms, images which seem to tell of larger forces at work. I also read a range of local history books borrowed from the local library. I had several long conversations with local taxi drivers about the area. I made two trips over a period of weeks at different times of the day, took photographs and also wrote a first draft of the poem in a café in the town. In Congleton I attempted to replicate this process but wasn't able to attend any local groups as I had in Runcorn due to time restraints. However I was taken to the local museum by library staff, for lunch with museum staff and local artists and for a walk onto a local beauty spot 'The Cloud'. On a return trip I went on a long solo exploratory walk without maps or plan. I like to try and find the edge of a place. I walked until almost lost and then found my way back to the town centre by remembering markers on the route, some of which appear in the poem. I also visited the local newspaper office where I bought a centenary issue, content from which features in the final poem. In both places I took photographs. These help to focus on the detail of the environment, though they are more about the process of looking. I don't use the content of the images in the poems. I use the images my imagination has stored and offers up in the process of composition.

Drawing on what I'd learnt in writing 'Arne's Progress' about presenting small actions as a focus, in this project I attempted to weave these actions together through an extended syntax running over several lines to visualise the towns as dynamic and counteract any stereotypes about small-town life. The details fuse in my mind's eye into an imaginative mental map, a topological vision of both places in which many of the historical elements were being played out simultaneously. I understand small towns are dynamic, focused, intense places. Cities offer a relief from the intimacy of the relations in small towns. These smaller communities have to constantly find ways to remake themselves and their relationships. I hoped a rebut-

tal of the stereotypical, insular idea of the local and of small towns
would be present in the final experience of the poems, both of which
conclude with contested future events; in Runcorn the building of
the new Mersey Gateway bridge, in Congleton the development of
new housing estates. Nowhere stays the same for long. The lengths
of the lines are varied to produce the lilting energetic movement I
hear as important in drawing the audience/reader into the work.
Both poems make use of long clauses and longer sentences to suggest flexibility within cohesion: a movement and flux yet contained
within limits. I hope to create the rhetorical effect and affect of the
sensation of a movement within the line, asking the reader/listener
to make connections over an extended clausal sentence. In doing
this I hope they will experience the movement of thought required
to make the connections between apparently disjunctive elements
across time and space. I hope this encourages an extension of mind,
or at least a comfortable relationship with the openness required to
enter into that state. I did not wish to overly disrupt the listeners' experience by using overtly defamilarising techniques such as paratax-
is, as I understand the extension of mind to be an experience which
occurs when the reader/listener is relaxed and able to forgo their
psychological boundaries, often created as a defence against the reality of this experience. Creative thought occurs when the mind is
able to relax and shift into lateral connections. The imagination
is allowed to wander across the terrain of the poem and to make
connections without the need to control or define their meaning
within known relationships. The experience I am looking to invoke
in a reader/listener is that felt when walking alone in the woods or
the moment before waking, the state of immersion we feel when
making something with our hands, or even when in love. These
moments are the 'blended spaces' from which new material space
can emerge. Yet for that state to occur the reader/ listener must feel
safe and less protective of an individuated self. Space, as I argued

earlier is not a lack, just a differing energetic state. By changing this state we can offer routes into new ways of seeing.

In the poems for small towns I juxtapose a range of times and spaces but maintain syntactic order, even if it is stretched over an unconventional clausal structure. I need my rhetoric to multi-task. I must both draw-in and compel the reader/listener but also offer an extension into the new. The listening experience should be one of integration but also dynamism and surprise. I was not looking to de-familiarise the towns; Runcorn in particular suffers a range of social problems and I deliberately chose not to focus on these elements as they are already very familiar to the local audience. A local audience can desire to hear what it already knows but I suggest in these post-industrial days is often looking or needing something different. The local poetry of Edwin Waugh in nineteenth century Lancashire described the shared experiences of the mill workers and was read by thousands. The poetry of the identity politics of the 1980s sought to describe shared experiences and this is a valuable approach to writing in a locality. However I cannot replicate this commonality as I understand poetry writing as an emergent process. As my creative practice is informed by a non-dualistic material philosophy I have to account for what my imaginative practice is doing in a given context beyond political identification. If construed as producing more material space from material presence in differing states then poetic thought is differentiating energy not always producing sameness.

Therefore, I understand the local poet's role as producing alterity and otherness within and from the familiar. I argue for this via the notion of local poetics presented throughout this thesis. A poem is doing something active within the matrix of material processes. Understanding this is key to the successful practice of a local poetics. The local poet is producing new space from the pressures which are conterminously producing the material realm. The local poet is extending this space to provide more opportunity for the movement of energy into new forms. The poetry will emerge from these pressures and will then offer something new in its perspective and position in relation to what is already known about the place. The local poet has to negotiate the tension of maintaining credibility and interest amongst the audience and the real work of the production of new perspectives. I use both the material and sensual properties of language to draw people into the work but not to produce identification, and I am also drawn to the folkloric for this reason. My interest in this genre emerged as a poetic strategy to manage the need to offer ambiguity yet also familiarity as these traditions suggest otherness while retaining a strong connection to place.

Both poems were well-received on rainy autumnal evenings. Feedback from audiences and staff was positive. 'Dusk Town' was published in two local newspapers and provisional plans were made to display it on the wall of the library. 'Congleton Tapestry' appeared in the 'Congleton Chronicle' followed by a positive article about the event. I was aware the Runcorn poem spoke more intimately about the town as I made use of memories shared with me by local people. In Congleton I had to focus more on the history, and the details of local people's lives as observed from distant perspective. However, this is perhaps the most honest perspective as I was only able to visit the town twice. I did learn a lot doing this work about the point of view needed to be taken by a 'local poet' and the ethical and communicative risks of appropriation. I developed my use of an extended poetic line and an understanding of how to imagine movement and place horizontally, to try and see the gaps between actions which can produce new actions; a bear running through a shopping precinct or a mermaid swimming through the shadows. I notice these details as when I imagine them I felt a pleasurable sense of release from the confines of the real. It is in the spatial boundaries, created by external pressures i.e. the contradictory need in this project to represent reality but also to say something new, where change or the unusual can emerge, as real extensive spaces, however fantastical.

ON THE FIRST MEETING OF THE RESEARCH GROUP: A POETICS

THE ghosts stole my diary. I asked to 'not be in control' and they responded, crept into the artist's studio, crawled under the table and pinched it from my open bag. I had marked out the time of our next meeting in my black moleskin elastic-bound diary. We discussed when and where, who should be invited, food and coffee-making (only hot water and ginger tea) and around me images on the studio wall convulsed silently, molar pencil sketches of modulations across time. Everyone was talking; we were leaning in. Some sat on the black leather sofa facing the white-framed eight- pane Georgian window and the view to the courtyard cafe below where, buying coffee earlier, the artistic director was meeting a storyteller to write another chapter in the history of the Gallery: the final chapter. I said to him, while asking for soya, that he should include a chapter on the ghosts. I heard them whisper excitedly when I said this, but he said he wrote about them a few years ago. I felt their rejection. Then I met a poet, a shaman, a performer, strangely - a crime novelist, and then the philosopher arrived running across the courtyard, framed by the open front door, unrecognisable, moving almost in slo-mo, but really running; a state I hadn't seen him in before outside the locked-down quadrant of our institutional frame.

When we spoke about dates for our next meeting, I heard laughter, a rumbling, a cackle and shift in the papers on the desk. *O Limina, here we are*, they didn't say. The steps outside the studio were grey and smooth, slippery, as I carried my tray of half-eaten sandwich and cold coffee in one hand, tried to keep up with everyone leaving, when I wanted us to stay in the room and talk forever, and no time to ever catch us there as the bricks on the wall scrambled a little, and on the stairs, small thin hands on the banister, the children ran, orphan children, too totally liminal; identity drawn from their white starched shirts and creased skirts and their faces aghast at our chat, and in their hands my diary carried on a velvet cushion like a sacrificed head to be torn to shreds with their fierce eyes and angry teeth.

*

Concepts are static; framed pictures on a shady wall. They hold meanings like a pint of water; a river poured into a vase. They re-present, make present what is lost. But what if the subject was mobile, never found or lost, never known? A poetic image can bring itself to you in your mind's eye: imagine. Then it fades to something else, into you; water seeping into skin, porous, yours. O, lovely soggy human brain, rinsing, straining, malleably-made. Beware concepts that restrain. *Into the ocean and into the rock. Under, please, go under.* Do not be captured, boxed. 'No ideas but in things,' said Carlos Williams. Also, in imaginings? A voice is a thing; it is heard, in the world. Conversation is not empiricism, a reduction, but recognition of the action of things that roar: are unstable. There is no representation which does not include a death.

"We all want to stay alive," say the ghosts on the stairs outside the studio. One is sat on the step, my diary in its hands, but shredded, torn into ringlets which hang like ivy over pale fingers.

"Why do you do this to time?" She stares accusingly as I stand at the base of the steps. They look down at me in contempt. A girl raises an arm and a slither falls to the floor. "This is how time moves. You capture it, you are a fool. Time is stronger and will rebel. It loops over and out of your bones and skin, your infections and your swollen ears. Are you listening?"

"Not really. I hear louder voices. I submitted to the living and their noise."

"They'll break you in two with their demands. You must listen to silences and what is arriving. Don't do this in concepts but in actions; in a moment that reaches into time and stirs the waves."

"We aren't metaphors," they say, as they walk up the stairs. "Are you not words?" I call after.

"No, not words. They belong to you. We are objects you apply them to. In doing so, you change us. We are objects under observation and we speak back when you address us."

I watch them become mouths, then outlines, then dust.

*

An 'I' in a poem is not a subject, although we might call it that. 'I' does not refer to a neat identity, but is a place-holder for a mutable point-of-view, a pair of ears through which to navigate the space of the poem, through which to follow syntax and to be led into the meaning, the newly opened space; a clearing; limina.

Remember something will always be leaving.

'I' is a poet, only as far as a poet is role-play, a performed act, an emptying of the self into which the world seeps and flows. The poet uses words to restructure the edges of what is known.

*

This sense of threat is receding. I went to the doctor's surgery and spent two hours waiting for my turn, wrapped in a wool coat and thick black scarf and the doctor said, when asked about the cause, he didn't believe in the word 'stress'. We paused. "Over-work," I offered. He had arrived earlier on his bike, a little rustled, a surgery full of bodies in need of care. And on the way home I cried in relief, not just for the diagnosis, but for the reassurance of being heard; *I must think of your health.*

As I cried my body did some thinking. The pressure in my head released, though I could not speak it until days after. To recuperate means, 'to recover or regain something lost or hidden.' The self-disciplining thoughts continued; guilt, a sense of threat and aggression, of my vulnerability known like a whip in a master's hand or threat of sanctions. The 'sin' I must not commit is to loose myself, not be action, not be productive, to not be in control. I must know what's happening: *the neo-liberal self must always be responsible. If you break this rule, you will have your privileges revoked.*

But what about the ghosts: this archaic me, this older, never-been-modern thinking body and her ruffled silences. How is she to live without being torn in two?

'JOURNEYING THROUGH':
POETRY AS A WAY OF KNOWING

WHAT is there in the silence? The sea and the edges of the land, a desire to feel the comfort of the in-between, have it take me in its arms and away on the wind; or how the storm needs to cover and carry me up and away from the shoreline, how the salt of the sea needs to bathe me, how I am looking for something new in the sea salt but cannot find it; only the yawning exhaustion of what has been left behind, the residue of what has been taken. What can I see in the water today? A face floating on the surface, no depth, just a losing, a shimmering, a peeling away to find something not made and not certain, something not identified or even made of clay, but made of light and fluid like the ocean as it comes for me on the shore, wanting to walk into its arms and not have to manage the walls of a self, always finding her in need of protection, yet too firmly held. Am I going to the sea today?

O definition, how violent you are.

The village of Llanrhidian on the Gower Peninsula rises towards me, a place I have never been before though my DNA lies somewhere in the churchyard—Rev. George Edgar Rees, 1812–1895. How did he become me?

I am here to research my father's family as I have inherited the Rees archive of diaries, vicars' ledgers, paintings, photos, and a large Victorian bible which also functions as a family tree; four generations of vicars beginning in Carmarthen, South Wales, via Worthing, Llanrhidian, Yorkshire, Nottingham, to Haslingden, Lancashire. One of my earliest memories is running around the wood- panelled rooms of St Peter's Vicarage then on the edge of the moors. I can remember the oval eyes in the grain of the wood. Today, I scramble over graves in the grounds of St Rhydian & St Illtyd's church, trying to tread softly and with respect. I do not find you, but I do write a draft of a poem, sitting on a wooden bench and looking out at the marsh.

I discover the location of your grave through serendipity; missed you when I came alone and still have not stood beside your grave under the yew tree. Friar Ardouin replied to my email asking about grave plots to say the church warden had just that week, following my exploratory visit, found a wooden wall plaque in a drawer with your name engraved upon it. He sends me a photo of your memorial stone. There it is clear as the present, beneath the yew tree like my grandparents always said. Friar Ardouin meditates beside you, plays his didgeridoo. He sends me a film of his playing there, the images blur—and it is mesmeric. Have we disturbed you?

O definition, how mercurial you are.

I am thinking about poetry and how I came to think about poetry, through this exploration of my ancestors. I look at your face in the digitised family photo from the 1880s, your druid's beard and wilful stare—patriarchal? I know that energy, or presume I do, 'The

Yew tree in the churchyard at Llanrhidian. Photo: Friar Ardouin

The engraved wall plaque. Photo: Friar Ardouin

force that through the green fuse drives the flower'.[1] Has something of this look become my poetry, almost without my consent?

And in the small village by the marsh in a harsh winter when the crops fail or illness arrives, how did you survive? What was needed then that we need now? Or need now to know?

I invoke you from my grandfather's handwritten notes. What did your father, the tallow chandler, learn in a turbulent Carmarthen during the Rebecca Riots, after migration from the village of Llanboidy, the place name a church settlement, early church, monastic? How far back can we go? Were you also looking for stability through change, a move away from struggle towards structure and security; form? Was your honouring of the force of life as a god a way to acknowledge the primary indeterminacy of all things; the Celtic idea of 'neart' as an energy that moves through the world to channel and balance the force; immanence not dialectic, becoming not identity?

You are also conduit, as am I.

Am I then, partly, a fallen-through-the-cracks-of-history subjectivity in which an old ontology survived in full sight of the new? Your journey from Carmarthenshire Independent Minister to Worthing to Oxford Movement Priest then back to Carmarthen and then Llanrhidian, a Welshman become English to become British, embodying a Celtic-Christian fluid immanence which became inarticulate, silenced by orthodoxy and colonial dominance, fell into muscle memory, dream. Until waiting again for a chink in history re-emerges through me as poetry from beyond the self—my own poetry's remarked upon 'otherliness'.

Was he a shaman? Or druid, unbeknownst?

I google Rev. W. D. Wood Rees to see what I can find, and I am astonished. The third entry is from *Phantasm of the Living*, a Victorian compendium of psychical research.[3] In it Wood Rees writes an account in a letter from 1885 of an event in October 1875 included in the chapter 'Dreams which may reasonably be regarded as Telepathic'. Wood Rees writes about the death of one of his Llanrhidian 'ministrations':

Rev. George Edgar Rees

I had a most vivid dream. I seemed to hear the voice of the above-named William Edwards calling me in earnest tones. In my dream I seemed to go to him, and saw him quite distinctly. I prayed with him and saw him die. When I awoke the dream seemed intensely real, so much so that I remarked the time, 3 a.m. in the morning. The next day I received a letter from my mother, with this P.S.: 'The bell is tolling; I fear poor William Edwards is dead.' On inquiry I find that he did die between 12 and 3; that he frequently expressed a wish that I was with him.

Wood Rees's brother Rev. Glyn Rees corroborates the tale. Wood Rees continues, 'I have sometimes dreamt I saw a person dying, and then heard they were ill.'

O definition, how immanent you are.

What poetry knows—if it is understood that there are no divisions between matter and mind, and man is not at the centre of all thought, that time and space are absolutely and literally in flux—is that 'vivid dreaming' or 'visioning' is a way to connect these worlds, to find activity across time and space. In writing this essay, I am re-imagining and connecting with what is thought lost and silent and giving resonances conceptual shape, communing with my ancestors. In writing a poem, I do the same but also give shape to embodied thought, to movement, to sensation. The poetic way of knowing is fulsome and non-reductive. The poem is often ahead of my conscious knowledge. A poem is not a representation but a virtual action, played out in the synapses, drawing on all the complex layers of matter and time which form the embodied mind. Poetry has always been something that I *do*, a form of interaction with the living world, a becoming, a journeying through.

O definition, how lively you are.

Rev. William Davidson Wood Rees

I have come to find you here in Barmby Moor, a commuter village outside York. The church-door rattles. This is the threshold
space I saw in the poem when you led me through this door and to
Llanrhidian. Now I sit here in your path. The door is locked today.
Your gravestones are listed as 'unstable' on the noticeboard by the
side of the gate. All four of you lie in the wild grasses, unmown I
presume to protect the stones, and unpassable. I squint to see the
names on the base of the stone, spot Gwen, Ellen, and then your
initials, W. D. The cross which would have marked you has fall-
en and lies to the right in the wheatgrass. I check closely to see
if you have a Celtic cross like Glyn, your bother, who lies parallel
to you just across the path which is slippery now with thunderous
rain. But the cross in the grass is simple and square-edged, *Anglo?*
Now some distance from the perpendicular, it waits for the time
when it is no longer forever and life transforms to light. Today,
however, is frequent warm showers of rain. My scramble to find
shelter in the what-I-thought-was-a-door led me to you. But the
door of the church is locked today and the only liminal place in
this well-kept village is this long grass flecked with yellow which I
watch intently as if I might find an answer to an unformed question.

O definition, how liminal you are.

I dreamt there was a woman outside my front door. She lunged at
me as I walked down the steps. She was gaunt, like an addict, had
cropped brown hair, pale skin. She was a Christian woman. I almost
recognised her. She entreated me to help her, but in a way which
seemed aggressive. When I refused, she lunged towards me and bit
my neck, just where the pain of my strained shoulder had begun. I
woke terrified, deep in the dark. A little later a heavy rain began,
or maybe it was already raining. Dawn arrived, rising from behind
the curtains, and lightened the room. Isaac, feline, leapt out of the

Memorial stone for Rev. Glyn Rees.

The Church at Barmby Moor

window into the rain but returned soon after and came, meowing, to sleep on the pillow behind my head. Has something been released? At lunchtime, I go to buy milk. On the front door is a handwritten sign. In black letters it says, 'Descend the steps with care, the middle step is broken'. I stand on the well-worn stone steps, and, although slippery, they are sturdy. Later, I try to find the broken step.

I cannot see it. It must have mended. When I open the front door again, the note has gone.

O definition, how more-than-human you are.

Late summer and I visit Gwydir Castle in the Conwy valley: a four-teenth-century stone manor house built by a Welsh prince. I stand in a grey hall which hosted bards. The house is damp and smells of time, ginger, dust. In spaces like this room, Welsh humanism was imagined, influenced by Renaissance Italy, but as historian John Davis writes, some bards still believed that their muse was 'of divine origin' and that the bards themselves were concerned that 'their dis-trust of the values of the Renaissance and of the printed book were signs of closed minds ...'. Maybe these court bards foresaw what was being lost, that the centring of the human male as a source of knowl-edge, his words powerful now on the pages of a printed book, would change the power relations between Man and the more-than-hu-man forever? In the Welsh language poetic tradition,

The Taliesin poems insist ... that such disenchantment is simply a way of settling down into a drab and reductive version of who we are and what our world is. We hardly need these days to underline the practical effects of this reductive approach, in the devastation of our environment, the brutal erosion of the rights and dignities of indige-nous peoples and the sheer frantic hollowness at the heart of the so-called developed world. In such a world, poetic imagination is no idle luxury: the poet is the person who is most intensely and fully aligned with the hidden energy and spirit that pervades our world, and we are poorer and less human, if we try to side-line or ignore this truth.[4]

In our current crisis of humanism, where the dominant definition of humanness is dissolving, we are both pre- *and* post-human. *The centre cannot hold.*[5] The porosity of time and space reveals glimpses of other worlds through the bushes, or unvalued forms of thought in the silent burrows of ourselves, dusty volumes now outdated; all knowledge as potential kept in waiting for the moment when time shifts irrelevance to necessity. Our storehouse is the space of our enchantment. This is what poetry knows.

O definition, how enchanted you are.

On a cold weekday afternoon, I go to the sea on the edge of the Wirral, the peninsula on which I was born. I sit at the red rocks and watch the tide, Hilbre Island, the Clwyd Hills beyond. I open my notebook and write a draft of some *thing*. This poem intercedes in the writing of this prose.

> ...I open my mouth in the body
> of a man, a voice like song licks
> out into the room—I am heavy-set, bearded
> but my tongue is gilt, a sword in the light
> as the men turn to me, eyeing up my
> pronouncements over the top of their
> beer-fug, burnt ash, residual blood
> on cloth, backdrop of damp, rain
> beyond the thick, grey stone thunders—
> horses in stables stamp steps over their straw beds,
> a peahen trembles back into the cover
> of the yew as the winds build
> as a procession of lights turns across the far garden,
> on the grassy terrace by the gate
> a torch held high struggles in the rain, but bright,
> a star which threads a string
> back towards the lead-lined,
> small-glazed window of the room
> in which the men are listening to this note

of song which is a myth circling from my lips
and back across the bay, to the mountain's top,
a kite's bold flight into the cloud, into rock
and sand at my feet on this August afternoon.

MARK-MAKING IN THE VIRTUAL

MATTER is, fluid, morphic. Being is, liquid, is a realist statement which informs how I understand writing and reading. We read and write from within being alive. The two acts are then interwoven stitches in one cloth.

Reading is writing as both are acts of interpretation. And what is interpretation? It is a shifting and rearrangement of space, a mark-making in the virtual. When we read ideas appear through association, are seen in space, are evoked and invoked, called up to the fluid realm of the virtual, vision, imagination. If this inner world is carved into as we might a cave wall, onto it we press our pigments or scratch out an image from a rock. If the virtual is a material, we skim stones over surfaces and ripples form.

From these associations breed associations, looping back to produce further connections. The touch of the keyboard, how I sit, my breath, my nervous system settled at home or destabilized by changes in air pressure, the hail on the window pane, who I am missing and who I have seen, all feed into loops of ideation—emerging abstractions I draw out; energy encoded into language forms in my mind's ear and eye. I read my own thoughts as I write, making judgements and following patterns I see forming through the process of writing. I read as a write. I shape and guide these ideas using the structure of syntax, which is a kind of governance, a legislator, and that which was in the world has become other, encoded in time awaiting another living body to read and interpret my reshaping of matter to continue the movement, the tag game, the dance.

And so I become a conduit, a conductor. Non-linear dynamics spill energy back out into the world which firstly filled me with its presence. I read the material: the context into which the writing will be published, the grain of the rock into which I shape the ink, the flow of the water I try to channel into sand to shape the word and leave a mark. The material also speaks to me. From our conversation we co-create, by looping and unfolding another capacity of matter. Together we make a boundary space where I am extended outside my brain, negotiating obstacles and tricky terrain by reading the world around my sentience in all its languages, human and not.

And so I am immersed within this liquid being, in an ethics of relation, maintaining the systems through call and response, extension and return; dynamics over which I have little or no control. Yet I guide the transformation as best I can. And reading is part of these exchanges of energy, part of the continuous activity of being alive. I make marks within the virtual which in turn mark me, or I am the marks for a moment as I lean into the water face first. I am other. Other is 'I'. The system connects, energy is transformed and I am away again into the river, streaming and looping, reading and writing, reading and writing

A LOCAL POETICS

MANY of the poems live in the locale around my home in the south of Liverpool, poems in which I am asking for a connection with a landscape supposedly mundane — the suburban road, the back yard and beyond to the cutting where trains run by. I understand all of these poems as 'local' — that is, made from interaction with limits of season and place. The Mersey's high tide ebbs a mile from my house, trains stream behind the garden wall, beech leaves shift, geese fly, my neighbours lock the front door as they leave our flats. The 80A bus passes over the bridge though I can only hear it. Dew settles. Carbon clogs up the sky. These transitions define reality. There is no stillness and there is no lack: each local movement has an impact on the other. And poetry is another of these transitions, dynamic — a charge, a movement of energy from one state to another via rhetoric and rhythm — then travelling back out again to the interior of the reader, or dispersed amongst an audience as sound and visualisation. In a world which is perpetually changing — in which there are no fixed states — the poet's work is to morph the forms we think with.

A poet's being is their material, a clay that's shaped through imagination into a vessel, a container of energy. The poet shares this shape around, passing the cup amongst the crowd. Everyone needs more or less water. No one needs the same amount. The poet must create work that can carry enough meaning to meet all these needs: so there is enough to go around. Dispersal is the communal function of a poet's work. Even a lyric is a communal form; in one way or another, everyone identifies with an 'I'.

Without connection our art-form becomes meaningless, since meaning-making is an act of alteration. The poet speaks with the river or the sea but she also continues this meaning- making process as she expands through language into her audience. Maybe, then, the audience for poetry should be thought of more as participants — joining in with the co-creation of meaning which is reading and interpretation. In my thinking and writing about poetry I use the term 'local poet' to describe these dynamic interactions: the poem becomes a collective re-imagining.

Working with other people to write the poems rebuilds the connection between poet and audience. If the poet understands that they are part of dynamic systems in a living world, part of natural and social processes, then we can understand that these interactions produce the poem. The poet is the connector and maker, the joiner-together of parts to create further structures which rest in turn on the processes below. But like any natural structure, poetry can bend in the wind or be subject to erosion. Sense is not static but alterable, changing shape almost as soon as it is made.

Working with processes involves imagining spatially, drawing on the varied tensions and energies that inhere in the local context, noticing them, retelling and interacting with their intentions. In the non-textual world, local context can offer form, a shape to work with that the poet can then re-form: again, the clay becomes the pot becomes clay. In the push and pull of my negotiations with reality the poems emerge, alive, hoping you will remake them, in love and in time.

*

What is the form that holds us? This is the space of the imagination, a common ground, a meeting place under the sky where we see and hear within all directions. The language of poetry — concrete, precise, resonant, metaphoric — opens out the land before us, like looking at a slope leading down to the sea. In the space created by poetic language we meet and we join, thinking differently, hypnotically, not with our critical minds but with our visual, spatial faculties. We are less enmeshed in 'my' perspective and more involved in the communal world-making of the poem. We are extended. This is an experience intangible but very real.

How we bring others into this space — not to disrupt or alienate but to include, but to transform ourselves a little, give our boundaries a stretch, roll them out and share the listening and the remaking — this is the work of poesis, the art of making.

Remembering the etymological roots for the name 'poet' returns the sense of change to the word, poetry as verb not noun, of dynamic moment when one thing becomes another. Our bodies alter moment to moment: thinking in tune with these shifts is a starting point for the local poet, sensed and situated deep inside reality and all its goings-on; speaking the changes is the challenge of the poem. In the lyric, verbs animate these moments in the self; another technique is to allow an energetic movement to emerge as music via the rhythm, harmony, narrative. Yet the narrative is not there to provide order — an explanation of events — but sequences elements for the pleasure of arranging time, long and short, fast and slow, up and down, in and out.

In a public context, such as writing to commission, the various pulls and pushes of the place and the people involved provide further structuring possibilities. What is the deadline? Who are the audience? Do they even like poetry? Often my poems emerge from projects in real places: 'Congleton Tapestry' was commissioned for a reading at Congleton Central Library in 2012, 'Mossley Hill' emerged from involvement with an academic research project on local food production in Liverpool; 'In Their Ears and In Their Eyes' is the result of an online collaboration about place, 'Protean Shifts' was written for performance on a barge; 'The Goat's Field' was written in a goat's field at the Centre for Alternative Technology, 'High Tide' is a song lyric written for folk singer Emily Portman.

Poetic form is not just patterns made with words but also the patterns made by people living in real places; it is like water threading through sand. The local poet always writes *with* the patterns she finds in the world. She takes them and reshapes them into something different: whatever is *now* required. These negotiations mean poems are produced which are fluvial: pushed and pulled out of the flows of the real into standing pools, temporal wells. By reinterpretation — listening and reading — the energy is released once more, pushing through the culverts in the culture into new shapes in someone else's life — a picture, a song, a fresh thought on the circumstances of the problem, a different mood than earlier in the day — brighter maybe, but more resonant and alive. This is how I experience good poetry, and it is what I hope to make for others, forms that can expand into other shapes and sense through the portal of the poem. In collaboration with other artists this process is intensified as the other voice or art-form offers further boundaries with which to negotiate, from which to make new outlines. The collaborative poem is that which can only be made by the dynamics of those people, in those circumstances, at that point in time.

And time is important to the local poet. It is the element which might run out. It must be ridden well, like a nervous horse, gently and with grace. Not too fast, not too slow; temporal concerns define all relational creative work. The flows and movement will be at different speeds — the project reading is on Monday, the artist needs the text by today, there is paperwork, o so much paperwork, the rain won't stop but the trains still pour through, blackbirds shrill, geese fly south, carriages with horses line the street in 1900, the first steam trains roll by, steam in the cutting, past and future become entwined, which is first and which is second we do not know.

Like stars flung across space from all angles
      the local poet catches a glimpse of bright tails
          lighting the night sky
              as gas burns out to black.

GOING VERY BIRD-LIKE: THINKING WITH THE NATIONAL POETRY LIBRARY

A sweltering summer's day deep in central London. The Thames hasn't offered much respite, the embankment bridge to the south bank laid me bare to the heat and the city streets scorch. Children play in the water fountain and a father and son talk in the cafe about how to best care for Mother—should she go into a home? Is she in danger living on her own?

And I am here at the Royal Festival Hall to think about poetry and communities though all I want from others today is solitude and shade. Out-of-place and down-south, I am always bewildered by London, so many people, so little time it seems. I start to fracture, become the couple arguing, or a student newly-arrived or a fantasy Bloomsbury poet of little renown walking the backstreet squares.

I nip into Foyles to check out the latest collections - poets of the 'London scene'. Do I like their words? How do they speak to me? Can I listen? And I enter the library, out-of-breath from the stairs, my dissolute self overheated and dripping away. I trawl through the magazines. Do these voices speak to me? What do they have to say? Poetry is a forge for the making of the meaning of selves and of groups of selves. We needs I, and I is always we. I've come from Liverpool to write about poetry and communities in a library. I can sense a connection here; I must find it. When I came last, in January through fog and ice, I met with Chris, National Poetry Librarian and Jessica, the Digital Coordinator and we spoke about how the library is a public resource, how it is used by a wide range of groups, how it is open to all. During my PhD, I spent years thinking about how poets make connections, make the boundaries and also trouble them till they fall. Poets build new 'legislation' to use Shelley's word. As a poet working in communities, I've seen this process in action many times. How meanings emerge; and to emerge they must be lost and re-made. In imagination, in refilling our emptying selves, poets do this work.

I make notes. Pascal the Assistant Librarian shows me around, helps me understand the history and work of the collection. The National Poetry Library (NPL) was established in 1953 as a result of the post-war settlement, the ambitious period which saw the creation of the NHS, National Insurance, the Arts Council.

Literary critic John Hayward described 'its purpose is the simple task of helping the reader of poetry, and particularly the younger reader, to get into easier and closer touch with the published verse of his poetic contemporaries'.

The library collects works from poets writing in English and the intention is profoundly democratic, as shown by Hayward's 'easier' and 'closer'. If poetic voice here is understood as that of the individual, then the reader is thought to commune with the poet, to become close, to understand difference through its encounter. A further quote from Ted Hughes shows me something of the transformative powers of the library doing its work. When putting together his seminal collection *The Rattle Bag*, edited with Seamus Heaney,

Hughes wrote to the poet Adrian Mitchell:

This last week I was sitting every day in the Poetry Library at the Arts Council going through every book that showed any likelihood of producing a poem for that anthology... I was trekking for days through the densely packed Ys and the insuperably ranked Ws – going very birdlike over the tops of their heads for the most part... Very strange experience, squeezing every morning into modern poetry, and sitting there all curled up with a book over mouth deeply, then coming out in the five or six o'clock dark onto Piccadilly again

Hughes, with his characteristic physicality, shows us how he was 'trekking' and flying through the library, as if the act of reading so many multiple voices was a sort-of vision quest, a self lost and then found again back in the dusky urban London street.

The library is a space for the making of selves, of putting our faces in the water to see if we can still breath underneath. The boundaries that language makes, the structure, form and shape of poetry is like a pool we can lose ourselves within. We are neither totally free, nor caged but can lean on the edges to let go into the depth. To let go, there must be someone to catch us, some form to take our shape for a while.

The NPL collection is not without its rules; any library is in the business of categorization and curation. Choices and responsible decisions must be made about which books are included, who is included. In the guidelines for 'unsolicited acquisitions' the librarians describe how they attempt to filter the many poetries now circulating in our culture. They advocate for reading 'over 100 contemporary poetry collections' before submitting one's own. 'This is the way to be sure you're creating something individual. All poets spark off and inspire each other, sharing forms and themes, but no committed poet wants to sound/read like a copy of another.' Indeed! And there it is again, the paradox of being a self in a group, or a group of selves. Individuality emerges from variety and in turn produces further individuality. And on…

And now, in this current moment, as we deconstruct our group identities, we also need to make communalities anew in order to know ourselves in the world. The current Instagram Poetry exhibition *(now finished)* shows this need in full tilt – the anxiety of being a self online, of seeking new rules. The aphorisms of Rupi Kaur elicit a feeling of safety, of knowing something fixed and sold in the face of flux, of identifying with a voice and with others in that fixity - of belonging.

These Instagram poems are asking for likes and to be liked. 'The way I hid in the bathroom because alone is closer to you' writes @ anon_sense on a photo of a plughole. 'Always lying to MYSELF.' a four word poem by @ernfariswrites. These poems want affirmation that their suffering self really does exist. And this is another, very human, paradox of contemporary poetry communities. All its voices, its defiant individualists like to meet and talk and gossip, often searching for more rules or boundaries to push against, to define themselves and to make themselves solid.

At 2:30pm I meet the London Haiku Group during their lunch break. We meet in the foyer to the library. Coming together to critique and share their haiku, the society all agreed they were indeed 'perfectionists'. Five, seven, five syllables makes for a baggy poem. Why use so many words? Why such lack of refinement, such lack of discipline?

I learn from Pascal that the NPL holds a busy children's session (Rug Rhymes) on a Friday and eight poetry groups meet regularly at the library - Tideway Poets, the Arvon Young Poets - to discuss their poetry, that is to discuss the making of selves in relation to others. Poetry will always pull in both directions, defining our experience whilst deconstructing it. For experience itself is never static but as alive as our need to know a self, in order to know the selves of others.

ON WRITING A POEM

IT'S the norm today to know that poetry can be found in many forms of writing; can be recognised in literature that aspires to further complexity, rather than an overly literal or reductive notion of truth. But this 'I' that does the talking, what and who is she? I am being mindfully disingenuous, of course, but this porous 'I' is the start of all my poems, indeed my poetics. She blurs her way into the world and it into her; the poems emerge from this altered state of mind.

So, a poem begins in an inarticulate feeling, often in my stomach, a sense of something moving nearby. Indeed, matter itself is unstable, and the world is alive so this isn't a fantastical notion. To recognise this sensation, I often write in situ, in a location. Recently, this has been at holy wells, the park, a corner of the street, the back yard; anywhere that speaks. You'll notice I stretch the idea of speaking here also. Thinking is embodied, so these intuitions are communication. My work as a poet is to use my desire to articulate, to do, well just that – to find words for what needs to speak.

And the words come by listening. I do think the poet is a conduit, understood not necessarily in mystical terms, but in the philosophical tradition of new-material or post-human thought. Immanent living matter swirls through us all constantly, indeed this is what we are. And if poetry is understood as a mode of knowing, the poet then thinks by opening to these energies and moving them into another state: words. Form and sound pattern are then important here. The constraint of the brevity of a poem (even a long poem), the rhythms and the sounds patterns, produce a focus, an improper 'self-hypnosis' which allows the energy to reshape into further rhythm, figuration, and emotional affect.

If poets keep close to this dynamic reality, then they write poetry. Much technique is then needed; practice in improvisation, careful editing, responses from readers or other poets. The finished poem can take months to sculpt. But the first draft, written by hand in a notebook in reaction to vital experience, if I've been listening with care, will always hold an energetic impulse. Knowing this impulse is an art in itself and requires intuition and some courage; often poems manifest in a particular image, or musical quality to the sound patterning, more recently dialogue and voices; turning the unseen into language requires thought, literary knowledge, and critical reason.

So, how I write a poem, is how I think, on a good day, in non-linear, fervent connections, spacial and expansive. Poetry is not representational thought, but thinking understood as ethical, embodied action. And poems begin in the reality of our being part of a constantly shifting, complex ecological relation to which we should all attune our bodies.

Do listen to the poets. The best of them have been doing this work since humanity found the words we needed to evolve. Please do pay attention.

STONE TO SAND:
A POSTHUMAN LYRIC 'I'?

'When I think of "the human", I don't settle my gaze on the anthropomorphic forms we habitually imagine as representative of what it means to be human. Instead, I notice patterns, fields, web-like connections, thresholds, processes, and multi-species arrangements'
— *Bayo Akomolafe*

FROM the summit of Helsby Hill, a sandstone crag and Iron Age hillfort, on the border between Cheshire and Merseyside, I stand and stare across the river as it flows to the estuary. Water scrapes through this geology, furrowing out a route within the Mersey basin; these crags formed of sedimentary sandstone laid down millions of years ago, now populated by retirees and commuters, workers at Stanlow oil refinery, ancient-city-esque in the distance. The white roofs of the shipyard like standing stones at Birkenhead, the town I grew up in; and beyond are the Welsh hills I gaze out onto from the park near my home in Liverpool, and I travel along on my way to the sea and the sacred well where I sit quietly, hermit-like under a grey sky. But that is beyond this horizon which is like a bowl into which to pour a life. What is held in the estuary speaks loudly of my existence, and of routes travelled, under, over, now up, and still to look out at the future and the past.

On the world's first railway line, I travel out of sight to Manchester, and also there I go over the Runcorn bridge to the south and beyond. From Speke airport, a plane takes off, and I look out of its window and down at the hill and at myself at school on the Wirral, cross country running at Rock Ferry on the edge of the river; away I go into the clouds and Europe. There I am on a hovercraft to Dublin, in a mini-bus into Snowdonia but also returning in a loop of silvery trails to this spot, looking out at shifting materials that made me.

*

I write this essay as a poet, not as a critic, from inside creative process and not at a distance from it. Sections of prose accrete here over a period of years. I do this as I want to acknowledge and honour knowledge first encountered in the world beyond language, in what is more-than-human. There is knowledge to be found in the relationship between word and world often overlooked by readers and poets alike. A preoccupation with the human social experience fails to recognise the threshold interactions beyond the human realm and how, indeed, these generate our humanness as a thinking individual separate from its environment. Anthropocentricity is, paradoxically, always a retort from the unavoidable encounter with the more-than-human. Our encounters with the generative forces of the world are where poetry arises, poetry understood here as poesis, as a moment of emergence, born of a conversation between the animate material world – tree, hill, plant, animal, river – using poetic imagination, that long maligned capacity for inhabiting a place without entering an extractive relation with it. The first moment of poetic creation is this communication which occurs as bodily thought, as a pictured mind.

The world speaks in its own language or rhythms, patterns, shadows, textures, sounds and smells, as a movement, gesture and touch. Engaging with this living cosmos as living asks that the poet first listens and experiences, moves with, silently stretching up, around and under the weaving movements of experience. These affordances, the possibilities offered to a creature in relation to other creatures, the space which becomes available for the poet in this dynamic, generates energy in the nervous system and compels the poet to speak.

This transmutation of energy continues to travel, though in more moderated form, into the crafting of a poem. As a poet composes, revises, reinvents, new constellations of meaning arise in relation to the differing components of a poetic language. Clusters of associations arise in the metaphors or adjectives, verbs can be sought which are active, changes to rhythmical patterns suggest new routes forward. The more the poet attunes to the affordance of their writing, the more likely that something unexpected will emerge. The poem can then write itself. The relations between the parts form a coherency and take on shape in poetic devices and the structures of syntax. A poem is guided into existence through the energetic intervention of the more-than-human.

*

Every concept laden upon lyricism smothers the delicacy of poetry's emergent thought. Writing prose about poetry is then a risky activity. Much damage can be done to the relation between mind and body in the poet if the thinking self petrifies into certainty. Supple flexibility is what is needed to dance with the more-than-human, as is metaphor to lift human minds out of the dangers of literalness. A poet is Janus-faced, Janus a god of transitions; the poet must speak to the more-than-human and to human social codes. Language as shared understanding then become important as a crutch to lean on as the poet tries to navigate this communion so all beings can be included. Creative language then remains alive and not a subject of thought to be dismembered by further thought. Analysis can violate the relation if thought is not also understood as an encounter with a living creature; hunting poesis down and chopping up its body for your own consumption is a form of violence to the more-than-human which still resides in the liveliness of the language of the poem. Poesis can though be encountered, explored, resonated alongside, and this is the relation I wish to establish between this prose text and poetic experience.

*

Walking the Sandstone Trail along the ridge at Frodsham Hill, I enter a quarry where the sandstone was cut. Chisel marks and elegant cursive script are inscribed into the sandstone. The stone records these marks, yet this stone is soft, crumbly, and dissolves under pressure from the heat of my fingers as I rub red grit into the lines of my palm. The stone's softness means that this sandstone can only be used to build smaller houses, barns, walls. The vernacular architecture of Cheshire is formed by this affordance. The black and white half-timbered houses sit on large slabs on sandstone from these local quarries. The rusty outcrops lean over the path, an upturned sandy beach. Alan Garner, the writer, folklorist and life-long resident of Alderley Edge, another sandstone crag east of Helsby writes, 'that its long history and prehistory make it unsafe at times. It is physically and emotionally dangerous. No one born to the Edge questions that, and we show it a proper respect.' (Garner, p.4) The land's porosity will immerse you and not let you go. As I walk on, I feel my body disappearing, becoming particle, molecular and gritty; it is a pleasant sensation and welcome, like being in the sea, muscles absorbing salt. Here I am absorbing sandstone, its craggy redness, exfoliating and rough, graining on my skin which is sand and then stone as I am outstretched now, star-shaped, my face against the outcrop, half-human and half- hillside, materialising.

*

Matter is animate as it is indeterminate. Matter is not a coherent, fixed substance but source of potential, here and not here. Matter is the magical potion in the cauldron in the mythic birth of the Welsh bard Taliesin who, on swallowing the liquid by accident gains knowledge and wisdom alongside the ability to change shape and become a rabbit, an otter, bird and corn, pursued by his mother, the witch, Ceridwen who swallows the corn and rebirths him.

Subjectivity inhabits indeterminate matter, mutability becoming a source of potential, becoming alongside and through an 'I' which only describes a partial aspect of the subject, whilst its body, a complex mutable system, and its relation to the environment of this habitation, also contributes meaningfully to its constitution. All 'I's are 'they'. All 'I's include the more-than-human. Lyric poetry reveals this onto-epistemological truth as in the construction of poetic voice in rhetoric on a page, the figure of 'I' opens into the typological gash that it is, a connection of dimensions. Posthuman poetics reads the 'I' always as this multiplicity and not the bounded subject conventionally represented as a unitary, self-knowing subject, standing alone on the page.

*

A few weeks after walking on Helsby Hill, I travel to Egremont, Wallasey at the river mouth, an elegant, if aged, Victorian seaside promenade. Standing on the sand on the Mersey riverbed, I look back at the crags, just about visible in the distance. Between lies Liverpool, my home and history and the context for many of my poems. My poetry is bookended by the imaginary line from the crags to the sands.

This essay exists in space as well as time of your reading, on an unfolding plane of connections which morph and erode as I write, and you read. Texts are not easily cut away from the material and context which produced them, to be held in aspic. When texts are relocated, they take on a new form. There is no going back.

As I write this prose, I do not preserve thought here but allow thoughts to recalibrate their meanings in relation to the broader context: crag becomes sand, sand is precipice, stone to sand. What holds thought together is not an abstract linear argument dependant only on human logic, but space and time itself and all the forces from which these ideas and images emerge; all texts are mycelium grown from a complex web of activity, politics, place and time.

This latter point is important to make overtly. Literary culture still understands poetry as originating in a unitary human subject. The subject in this contemporary formulation is always a conscious mind with a knowable identity which could articulate its knowable voice and experience ever so more clearly if only it used language and the conventions of literature with more control. Though crafted writing is essential to a posthuman poetic practice to enable the transformation of material energy into sense, as a poem is only a temporary resting place on a long journey, part of a process of communication and transformation, a more accurate and adequate theoretical understanding of subjectivity is required to think about contemporary poetry, one which acknowledges poet as shapeshifter and conduit. The poem passes through me as poet. I do not own it. It never belonged to me.

*

To enable this movement, a space must be created in the virtual realm, in the otherworld. This is the real space of imagination, not a fantasy, but spatial visioning. Within this state of mind, the poet can see from all perspectives, or like a ghost seep and move between positions and subjectivities, to occupy many spaces simultaneously. This perception is not empathy, as that modality replicates human emotion, but a fluidity, more like dreaming, which enables a poet to seek the full picture from multiple angles, the active panorama of a multivalent experience of space and time.

I've always been drawn to poetry as a psychic edgeland, less governed by the observable rules of time and space then a mythic and mutable space where I become many, becomes perspectival. In *How Forests Think*, anthropologist Eduardo Kohn remakes his discipline to encompass a broader perspective, one which includes the more-than-human and living forest in an ontology which does not focus solely on the human. He defines this as a perspectivism, an epistemology which knows from all viewpoints including the forest. Kohn learns this way of seeing from the Runa people of the Amazon. He writes,

> a perspectival stance is certainly a practical tool…but it also affords something else. It allows one to linger in the space where, like a shaman, one can be simultaneously aware of both viewpoints as well as how they are connected by something greater that… suddenly encompasses them. (Kohn, 97)

As a distinctive philosophy which has emerged in the Amazon rainforest, this perception cannot be directly applied to western culture. Yet learning from indigenous thought can create resonances, and a reappraisal of suppressed Western cultural practices which can be reworked for the present.

Within British poetic history, there still exists I speculate, a residual perspectivism to be found in the traditional understandings of the poet's role in society, understood as a voice able to speak from multiple perspectives, either for a specific group or with the more-than-human. This bardic idea of poetic voice is found in Welsh and

Gaelic poetries, in the idea of the Bard, the Fili (meaning 'seer' in Old Gaelic) or in Old Norse, the Skald and in the practice of the West African Griot, in the 'Afro-diasporic knowledge systems', Jason Allen-Paisant describes in 'Animist Time and the White Anthropocene' and recognises as an alternative poetics. Are these residual pre-modern understandings of the role of the poet within a community with some poets offering social comment and moral guidance in the social realm, but others, and I am one of these poets, speaking *with* the more-than-human? Both practices involve not just empathy with an individual human subject but a broader immersion in the experience of a group, or indeed a place or environment, an engagement with a monistic ontology, an inclusion of all life in the being of the world, and therefore in the poem.

These are faint and suppressed notions of the poet as their ontology challenges our cultural notion of individual subjectivity, but they are present in Liverpool, in its diverse and colonising history, in its radical politics and religious heritages. It is the concept of the poet I have always written within. From Merseyside and its history of migration, colonisation and transport; as a portal between countries and cultures, I understand poetic voice as a contemporary bardic voice, a performative 'I', yet not speaking for the group but speaking *with* the place, social context, more-than-human, placing an emphasis on becoming other, and of moving betwixt and between human and nature, class and gender norms. In this context, the lyric 'I' as I understand it is not a representation of voice or stable identity, but an invocation of a voice which can speak *with* the energies of the world, translating them into the present and continuing their life. The 'I' of my poems is in a state of becoming, seeking to see from all dimensions through one subjectivity. When I write in the first person in a poem, I invoke, I don't represent.

I define then the constitution of the lyric voice as perspectival, a non-unitary subjectivity existing within an apparently singular voice, a performance of unity, a paradox difficult to voice in prose. This premodern, resonant poetics is therefore also posthuman. This most contemporary of intellectual terms seeks to describe a subjectivity as it roots and swells, climbs and composts under the material forces and affordances of technological and climate change.

*

I stand on the edge of Bidston Hill looking out at the post-industrial landscape of East Wirral, the docks soon to be regenerated with flats and a linear park in the derelict railway, and over past the Mersey to the Liverpool skyline, the collective memory of ocean liners debarkation to America and ships sailing with goods bought with the monies made from enslaving people from Africa. This heathland hill was owned by the Vyner family, descendants of Earl Robert Vyner, goldsmith and creator of the Crown Jewels. In the 1890s, the hill was bought by public conscription, monies raised by local residents and funds from the Birkenhead corporation. The windmill has an engraved plaque amongst the lichen-grey pebbledash which reads that Bidston Hill

> ... must always be used
> as an open space and place of public
> recreation, and must be preserved and
> maintained as far as possible in
> its present wild and natural condition,
> special care being given to the
> preservation of the trees, gorse, heath
> and heather and also of this windmill.

The growing Victorian docklands town of Birkenhead needed a wilderness, a pastoral escape, a space where subjects would not have their energy extracted from them for the benefit of capital. The hill is a short walk from the redbrick terraced streets. The windmill stands looming with its wooden sails tethered to the sandstone, and there is a thatched crofter's cottage at Tam O Shanter Urban Farm. Birkenhead is Scottish, built by Lairds. Behind me, the sandstone crag drops down towards the drained marshlands, a 1960s council estate, and through the treeline, I can see the Wirral coast and the sea rolling its way back to Ireland and the ferry, maybe, on the horizon. The Bidston ridge is the end of a sandstone escarpment which runs twenty miles from Helsby Hill. The sandstone carved into by Norse settlers to mark a sun goddess into this heathland. The stone carving is hidden now amongst the gorse and silver birch.

I used to sit on my soft-furred dark dun horse, Duncan, as a teenager in the 1990s, after riding up through the steep woods from Eleanor Road, and would watch this view, so I know it from memory. I write it from memory. To my left the sandstone, grand Bidston Observatory, where I once worked as a receptionist, sat in an empty corridor by a phone which never rang, is now an artistic research centre. The inland lighthouse no longer shines but the place is bright.

I watch as the sun goddess stands up from the rock, stretches her outline until she is a shadow, though sun-flecked, and she walks back along the track, as I ride alongside her years ago, listening for the moment the woods called my name, said 'Eleanor' on a spring evening after school, and I heard them, astonished, but then spoke back, 'yes', I called to the woods, 'yes?'

*

Writing a lyric voice is not an act of reinforcing a preexisting identity in a social group. Rather it is an interlocution with the spaces of the world. The encounter is not the meeting of two clear boundaries, two movements of energetic force but an opening outward of both parties (the term here rightly noting the multiplicity of our interiority) and a diffusing of the subject position into the coterminous space of the other. The space is only held in form in time through relation to other stabilising forces. It is ground down and it is rebuilt, appearing and disappearing in relation to that which crafts its material. The more-than-human world is constitutive of the lyric voice as it is in these moments of encounter that the poet communes at the edges of a social self, going to the edge of the definition of human and reaching an arm over into the otherworld.

The otherworld should always be approached with care and craft. I am not describing an involuntary process here, an illness or mistake, but an imaginative experience produced by the technique of poetry writing. The concentration and mental agility required to write poetry produces new spaces in the emergent material of consciousness which can be moved within and through. This special opening, if traversed with care, can lead the poet into perceptions beyond their own immediate awareness. The lyric voice is a letting go of identity and a corralling of the material properties of language, association and metaphor especially, to follow emergent images and associative logics, to have a look around in potenia! Writing poetry is then a practice in misalignment with current cultural notions of the individual. A poet does need to 'have a voice', or a single identification with a clear definition of place or group but listen for a voice made *with* the world and *with* the awareness of the multiplicity of selfhood. Indeed, this listening is a disidentification. Poets are not speaking for themselves. The desire to share a poetry comes from a need to maintain alternative and adjunct spaces to settled cultural conventions offering a portal to encounters with the otherworld and all its poiesis.

*

Yet the spaciousness of human subjectivity is being mined and extracted. The complex dimensions of human interiority have become resources to be quarried away to be sold for profit. Just as the hill was quarried to build new structures, the human subject is now the resource under erosion as part of this new iteration of the industrial revolution. This time around it is our thoughts and perceptions which are capitalised upon. The logical end point of the 'cultural industries' is the mining and extraction of the spaciousness of inner life. In *Liverpool and the Unmaking of Britain* historian Sam Wetherell offers a history of the recent past, of the years of my childhood, in the 80s and 90s on Merseyside, a place he recognises is faced with economic obsolescence. (Wetherell, 2025). Indeed, I have always been haunted by the phrase 'managed decline' to describe my future. In such a politics it becomes reasonable to 'be a poet' and create one's own spaces both as a protection from decline, as something that I can own, but also as a recognition of the potential of open spaces, of docklands left to rust and an inner landscape which is also an edgeland. In such a place, a new understanding of time and space is required, not the false logic of an extractive 'progressive' modernity and not a regressive return to an also false linear historical narrative. The river runs to the sea, but it also flows into tributaries, underground pools, the boxed-in and walled-up holding bay of the still waters of the docklands.

The wind is blowing in from the sea. The seedlings in the pots in my back yard are warming in the imported soil. Complexity inside selfhood, depth and dimension must be maintained. It cannot be reduced to a knowable phenomenon but must remain porous, arriving in the moment, unidentified. We should not know who we are so we can know others in relation as they appear blinking in the daylight. Poetry is the experience of finding spaces within spaces, of not being hemmed in by literal or reductive reason but offering inside the lyric voice a resonance of perspective. I draw a parallel between the spaces found in poetic thought and the spaces of the material world which are being extracted by the current economic model. The extraction of the self is also the extraction of property value by an unregulated economy, these definitions owned and sold to create asset wealth for a few who dominate the economy and politics of this contemporary moment. The contemporary radicalism of the art-form of poetry is a refusal to be named, to be recognised and identified and to be sold, all happening within the paradox of the posthuman convergence of multiple extractions of wealth and power. How we stop the trade in subjectivity is a question pertinent to the life of a poet in the deindustrialised and decolonising city of Liverpool and one I cannot answer here. The lyric voice holds itself within time, through the ecological flows of ontological processes, moves with these into speech but, as with all life, these processes should never be for sale, for their value exceeds all human definition.

BIBLIOGRAPHY FOR 'EYES IN THE WOOD'

Braidotti, Rosi, (2021) *Posthuman Feminism*, Cambridge: PolityPress.

Braidotti and Bignall (ed), (2019) *Posthuman Ecologies, Complexity and Process after Deleuze*, London: Rowman & Littlefield.

Davies, John, (2007) *A History of Wales*, London: Penguin.

Dubliet, Alex, (2018) *The Self-Emptying Subject*, New York: Fordham University Press.

Frick, Dr, (2011) *Eastham Ferry*. Available at: http://oldwirral.net/ eastham_ferry.html (Accessed: 13/04/22).

Graeber and Wengrow, (2022) *The Dawn of Everything, A New History of Humanity*, London: AllenLane.

Ingold, Tim, (2022) *Imagining for Real, Essays on Creation, Attention and Correspondence*, London: Routledge.

Ingold, Tim, (2011) 'The Textility of Making', *Being Alive: Essays on Movement, Knowledge and Description*. London: Routledge.

Ndlovu, S. Duduzile, (Ed), (2021) *Moving Words: Poetry as/in Research*, York: York Tree Publications.

Rees, Paul, (2020) Rees Family Tree. Available at: https://www. myheritage.com/site- 139198391/rees1 (Accessed: 13/04/22).

Wood-Rees, W. Rev. (1911) *A History of Barmby Moor*, Pocklington: W. & C. Forth Printers.

Wood-Rees, W. Rev. (1900s various) *Miscellaneous Writings by W.D. Wood Rees*. Private Collection: Unpublished.

Wood-Rees, W. Rev. (1876) 'A Curate's Wedding Diary' Letter. Private Collection: Unpublished.

Williams, Sioned, (2022) Email to Eleanor Rees, 12 April 2022.

Writing in Situ locations:

Cressington Park Esplanade, Liverpool, L19 OPP

Sudley House Park, Mossley Hill Road, Aigburth L18 8BX

BIBLIOGRAPHY FOR 'JOURNEYING THROUGH'

Barad, Karen. 'After the End of the World: Entangled Nuclear Colonialism, Matters of Force, and the Material Force of Justice.' Public open lecture for the students of the Division of Philosophy, Art & Critical Thought of European Graduate School on 13 August 2019. Saas-Fee, Switzerland. http://www.egs.edu

Barad, Karen. *Meeting the Universe Halfway: Quantum Physics and the Entanglement of Matter and Meaning*. Durham: Duke University Press, 2007.

Braidotti, Rosi. *Posthuman Knowledge*. Cambridge: Polity Press, 2019.

Brown, S. J., P. Nockles, J. Pereiro and S. J. Brown (2017). Ireland, Wales, and Scotland, Oxford University Press.

Davies, John. *A History of Wales*. London: Penguin, 2007.

de Castro, Eduardo Viveiros, ed. *Cannibal Metaphysics: For a Post-structural Anthropology*, translated by Peter Skafish. Minneapolis: Univocal, 2014.

Duinn, Seán Ó. *Where Three Streams Meet: Celtic Spirituality*. Dublin, Columba Press, 2000.

Gurney, Edmund, Frederic Myers, and Frank Podmore, eds. *Phantasms of the Living* (Cambridge

Library Collection - Spiritualism and Esoteric Knowledge). Cambridge: Cambridge University Press, 2011.

Gutch, Eliza. *Examples of Printed Folk-lore Concerning the East Riding of Yorkshire*. Nendeln, Liechtenstein: Kraus Reprint, 1967.

Hutton, Ronald. *Pagan Britain*. New Haven: Yale University Press, 2014.

Kohn, Eduardo. *How Forests Think: Toward an Anthropology Beyond the Human*. Berkeley: University of California Press, 2013.

Rees, Alwyn, and Brinley Rees. *Celtic Heritage: Ancient Tradition in Ireland and Wales*. London: Thames & Hudson Limited, 1989.

Skinner, Simon Andrew. *Tractarians and the 'Condition of England': The Social and Political Thought of the Oxford Movement*. Oxford: Clarendon Press, 2004.

Thomas, Dylan. *The Dylan Thomas Omnibus*, London, Orion Books, 1995.

Skoulding, Zoë. Underground Rivers: Notes Towards a Zoepoetics. In *Atlantic Drift: An Anthology of Poetry and Poetics*, edited by James Byrne and Robert Sheppard. Todmorden, UK: Arc Publications, 2017.

Williams, Rowan, and Gwyneth Lewis. *The Book of Taliesin: Poems of Warfare and Praise in an Enchanted Britain.* London: Penguin, 2019.

Wood-Rees, William Davidson. *A History of Barmby Moor from Prehistoric Times.* Pocklington W. & C. Forth, 1911.

Yeats, William Butler. 'The Second Coming'. In *Selected Poems*, edited by Timothy Webb, London, UK: Penguin Classics, 2000.

REFERENCES FOR 'STONE TO SAND':

Akomolafe, Bayo, Twitter @BayoAkomolafe: (Accessed. 17.03.23)

Allen-Paisant, Jason (2021) 'Animist Time and the White Anthropocene', *New Formations*, 2021(104 & 105), 30-49. https://doi.org/10.3898/NewF:104-105.02.2021

Braidotti, Rosi. *Posthuman Knowledge*. Cambridge: Polity Press, 2019.

Brownhill, John, M.A, A History of Old Parish of Bidston, Cheshire, 2023. Available at: vol 87 (1935) - A history of the old parish of Bidston, Cheshire - The Historic Society of Lancashire & Cheshire (hslc.org.uk) (Accessed: 17.02.23)

Garner, Alan, *The Voice that Thunders: Essays and Lectures*. London: Harvill Press, 1998.

Kohn, Edward, *How Forests Think: Toward an Anthropology Beyond the Human*. United Kingdom: University of California Press. 2013.

The Friends of Bidston Hill, 2023, Heritage. Available at: http://www.bidstonhill.org.uk/ (Accessed: 17.0.23).

Wetherell, Sam. *Liverpool and the Unmaking of Britain*. London: Bloomsbury, 2025.

ENDNOTES

[1] Thomas, *The Dylan Thomas Omnibus*.p.11

[2] Wood-Rees, *The History of Barmby Moor from Pre-historic Times*.p.15

[3] Gurney, Myers, and Podmore, *Phantasms of the Living*.

[4] Williams and Lewis, *The Book of Taliesin*.p.xvii

[5] Yeats. W.B., *Selected Poems*.p.124

ACKNOWLEDGEMENTS AND NOTES

Thanks are offered to the editors of these journals for the first publication of versions of these lyric essays and prose writings.

'Congleton Tapestry and Dusk Town': Writing *with* Small Towns', *Lighthouse Literary Journal*

Feature Essay Issue 6 Online Supplement. (Autumn 2014). Unavailable.

'Journeying Through': Poetry as a Way of Knowing, Ndlovu, D.S. (ed), Moving Words, Poetry In/As Research, York: York Tree Publications, 2021. Ebook. This essay has had limited distribution.

'The First Meeting of the Research Group', Lune Journal of Literary Misrule, Display (3), p. 124. Available at: https://lunejournal.org/03-display/ (03.20), 2017

'Going very birdlike': Reflections on Poetry and Community at The National Poetry Library', (2019), Available at https://www.national-poetrylibrary.org.uk/news-stories/going-very-birdlike

'On Writing a Poem', posted on September 17, 2019, Poetry Wales website.

'Preface to Riverine', Riverine, (2015), Norwich: Gatehouse Press. The essay presented here is a revised version of this text. Out of Print.

'Mark-Making in the Virtual', Sam Skinner and Nathan Jones (ed) The Act of Reading (2015), London/Liverpool: Torque Editions. Out of Print

With thanks also to Dave Ward, Dr Cornelia Gräbner, Dr Duduzile Ndlovu and the Limina Research Group, Liverpool Hope University.

Thanks also to the Arts and Humanities Research Council, University of Exeter, The Windows Project, Liverpool, From Cosmos to Genes: New Materialist Methodologies 2016, Crossing the Humanities, Natural, and Technosciences Training School, Charles University, Prague. EU cost action funded.

LAY OUT YOUR UNREST